# THE
# PROMISES
# OF JESUS

BIBLE VERSES OF HOPE AND STRENGTH

## MIKE NAPPA

GENERAL EDITOR

Our Daily Bread
Publishing™

*The Promises of Jesus: Bible Verses of Hope and Strength*
© 2020 by Our Daily Bread Publishing

Requests for permission to quote from this book should be directed to:
Permissions Department, Our Daily Bread Publishing
PO Box 3566, Grand Rapids, MI 49501
or contact us by email at permissionsdept@odb.org.

For a complete list of Bible translations used, and the respective permissions
statements of each copyright owner, please see page 189.

Interior design by Michael J. Williams

**Library of Congress Cataloging-in-Publication Data**

Names: Nappa, Mike, 1963- editor.
Title: The promises of Jesus : Bible verses of hope and strength / Mike
   Nappa, general editor.
Description: Grand Rapids, MI : Our Daily Bread Publishing, 2020. | Sum-
   mary: "This Scripture-based book looks specifically at the words of Jesus
   and provides the references so readers can dive deeper into the Word"--
   Provided by publisher.
Identifiers: LCCN 2020013095 | ISBN 9781640700529 (paperback)
Subjects: LCSH: Jesus Christ--Promises. | Bible. New Testament--Quotations.
Classification: LCC BT306 .P76 2020 | DDC 232.9/54--dc2 3
LC record available at https://lccn.loc.gov/2020013095

ISBN: 978-1-64070-052-9

Printed in the United States of America
21 22 23 24 25 26 27 / 8 7 6 5 4 3 2

# CONTENTS

# INTRODUCTION

## EXACTLY WHAT DID JESUS PROMISE YOU?

You've likely heard lots of sermons about Christ's promises, read lots of books, and maybe even prayed promises in your own words. But have you ever stopped to examine them for yourself? Taken time to read the words of Jesus himself, to discover to whom and for what each promise was made? Because, honestly, you can hardly swing a cat in the New Testament without hitting a time when Jesus makes a powerful promise.

*But are all those promises for you?*

That's what we set out to discover, and that's what this book is about.

We scoured through the Gospels and Acts, the New Testament letters, and even Revelation looking for those "red-letter" moments—the spoken words attributed to Christ himself. And every time Jesus made a statement of truth that (in our opinion) appeared to incorporate a promise within it, we asked the following three questions:

1. "Is this promise for everyone—for 'anyone who believes' or 'whosoever will'?"

If the answer was yes, then it went into the section of this book titled, "What Jesus Promised Everybody." These promises may have been spoken to individuals or groups, but what sets them apart is Jesus's generalized application of truth.

For instance, when Jesus said to Nicodemus, "whoever believes in him shall not perish but have eternal life" (John 3:16 NIV), He was speaking to an individual—but His application of that truth is clearly universal. So, it seems safe to assume that regardless of the people to whom these truths were originally spoken, these "whoever" kinds of promises are meant for you and me as much as they were meant for those to whom He first spoke.

2. "Is this promise for Jesus's disciples?"

If that answer was yes, then it went into the section of this book titled, "What Jesus Promised His Disciples." These promises were given directly to one or all of those in Jesus's inner circle—the twelve who followed Him before his death and resurrection. They are often characterized by the pronoun "you" or were prefaced with gospel-writer commentary indicating that Jesus was speaking truth directly to His disciples. For instance, when Jesus said in Matthew 16:28 (NLT), "Some standing here right now will not die before they see the Son of Man coming in his Kingdom," that seems to be a promise directed specifically to His twelve disciples.

The truths in this section are often-quoted, often-preached. Some are wonderful; others are quite frightening. These may be promises for you and me as well . . . or they may not be. It's possible that many of these promises are still for us today—and that some (or many?) of these were promises Jesus intended only for that specific group of men who were his most intimate, original followers. As you prayerfully read this section, perhaps you can determine if any of these promises belong to you—or perhaps it will take a little more study to figure this out.

3. "Is this promise for someone else completely?

If the answer to this last question was yes, that typically meant Jesus's promise was specific to some person or group with whom He was talking in that time. This would include, for instance, the promise to Martha that her brother would live again (John 11:23) the statement to Paul that he would be sent to the Gentiles (Acts 22:21). These kinds of promises have been collected into the section of this book titled, "What Jesus Promised Others." It doesn't seem likely that all, or even most, of these promises are for us today—but again, as you prayerfully read and study them you can determine if any belong to you.

### Now What?
Not everyone will agree with the specific selections of, or the category placement of, the Scriptures in this book. *That's okay.*

It should come as no surprise that this kind of parsing of biblical text sometimes invites loud, blustering arguments among denominational and theological types—particularly when Jesus is talking about the end times. So, let it be said plainly now that while we've tried to be comprehensive and consistent in our work, we also understand we can't be exhaustive or infallible, simply because there are (and will be) differences of opinion on what constitutes a promise of Jesus, whether a truth is just a "truth," or a "truth with a promise," and to whom a certain promise was originally given.

So please keep in mind that the compilation of this book was a human effort, not a divine endeavor, and it's perfectly fine if you disagree with a choice we've made in here. We've used our own judgment in regard to the curation and organization of the entries in this book—and we invite you to do the same as you read through this unique collection of Scriptures.

*Meanwhile . . .*

There are over 350 promises collected in this book. Other than the organizational framework described above, there is deliberately no commentary, no word study or interpretation, no assignment of a topical theme, no cross-references, no other "extra stuff" included in here. Just Jesus's promises—the red-letter moments only—and where you can find them in the Bible.

Here's what that means:

1. You can discover all the promises of Jesus in Scripture. Study them in context to see what they mean. Then prayerfully ask God for wisdom in applying these promises.

2. You can be encouraged each day by as many, or as few, promises from Jesus as are relevant to your life. Some days you may enjoy reading three, or five, or fifty! Other days there may be just one promise that you need—and you may need it every day for a week. Or a month. Or longer. The choice is up to you.

3. You can contemplate at your own pace some of the less-popular, harder-to-understand promises Jesus made. Yep, not everything Jesus promised was sunshine and roses. What will you do with those unpopular truths? You can prayerfully decide.

4. You and those around you can more easily discuss your thoughts on each promise of Jesus found in the New Testament. Some use this book as the starting point for a small group study. Others use it as a weekly or daily devotion with families. Regardless of how you use it, when you discuss this book with others you can all begin to verbalize and formalize what you understand and believe about Jesus's promises in the New Testament.

5. You can take to heart the words of Christ—and more easily share them with others in your world. Your coworker at the office, your granddaughter's choir teacher, your son's best friend down the road, your spouse, kids, and parents. Anyone who needs to hear from Jesus can hear His voice from you as you internalize and live out Christ's promises in the New Testament.

6. You can easily take your exploration of Christ's promises from this book right into God's Word—anytime, anywhere. Remember, Scripture references are provided for every single promise here, so keep your Bible nearby. When a promise intrigues you, or raises a question for you, or just makes you feel curious for more information, then we encourage you to check out that promise in greater context within the pages of your own Bible. When you do that, you can discover more about when and where Christ said these things and likely add to your understanding of that red-letter moment.

All right, then. This adventure is about to begin.

In here you'll explore, at your own pace, what really matters in your faith and life. In here you'll dig deeply into Scripture, you'll wrestle with truth and what it means for you today, right now, right here. You may even lose yourself in the pursuit of a greater understanding of Jesus's timeless, treasured promises. So I have to ask again:

*Are you ready?*

When you are, take a breath. Turn the page.

And let the adventure begin.

It's my prayer that you may meet Jesus personally, intimately, and frequently through His words collected in this book. Amen.

Mike Nappa, general editor

# PART 1

# WHAT JESUS PROMISED EVERYBODY

Man shall not live on bread alone, but on every word that comes from the mouth of God.

MATTHEW 4:4 NIV

Blessed are the poor in spirit: for theirs is the kingdom of heaven.

Matthew 5:3 KJV

Blessed are they that mourn: for they shall be comforted.

Matthew 5:4 KJV

Blessed are the humble, for they will inherit the earth.

Matthew 5:5 CSB

Blessed are those who hunger and thirst for righteousness, for they will be filled.

Matthew 5:6 CSB

Blessed are the merciful: for they shall obtain mercy.

Matthew 5:7 KJV

Blessed are the pure in heart: for they shall see God.

Matthew 5:8 KJV

Blessed are the peacemakers: for they shall be called the children of God.

Matthew 5:9 KJV

Blessed are those who are persecuted because of righteousness, for theirs is the kingdom of heaven.

Matthew 5:10 NIV

Don't misunderstand why I have come. I did not come to abolish the law of Moses or the writings of the prophets. No, I came to accomplish their purpose.

Matthew 5:17 NLT

Truly I tell you, until heaven and earth disappear, not the smallest letter, not the least stroke of a pen, will by any means disappear from the Law until everything is accomplished. Therefore anyone who sets aside one of the least of these commands and teaches others accordingly will be called least in the kingdom of heaven, but whoever practices and teaches these commands will be called great in the kingdom of heaven.

Matthew 5:18–19 NIV

He causes his sun to rise on the evil and the good, and sends rain on the righteous and the unrighteous.

Matthew 5:45 csb

No one can serve two masters, since either he will hate one and love the other, or he will be devoted to one and despise the other. You cannot serve both God and money.

Matthew 6:24 csb

For everyone who asks, receives. Everyone who seeks, finds. And to everyone who knocks, the door will be opened.

Matthew 7:8 nlt

If you then, being evil, know how to give good gifts to your children, how much more will your Father who is in heaven give what is good to those who ask Him!

Matthew 7:11 NASB

So in everything, do to others what you would have them do to you, for this sums up the Law and the Prophets.

Matthew 7:12 NIV

A good tree produces good fruit, and a bad tree produces bad fruit. A good tree can't produce bad fruit, and a bad tree can't produce good fruit.

Matthew 7:17–18 NLT

Therefore everyone who hears these words of Mine and acts on them, may be compared to a wise man who built his house on the rock. And the rain fell, and the floods came, and the winds blew and slammed against that house; and yet it did not fall, for it had been founded on the rock. Everyone who hears these words of Mine and does not act on them, will be like a foolish man who built his house on the sand. The rain fell, and the floods came, and the winds blew and slammed against that house; and it fell—and great was its fall.

Matthew 7:24–27 NASB

And I tell you this, that many Gentiles will come from all over the world—from east and west—and sit down with Abraham, Isaac, and Jacob at the feast in the Kingdom of Heaven.

Matthew 8:11 NLT

But I want you to know that the Son of Man has authority on earth to forgive sins.

Matthew 9:6 NIV

I am not come to call the righteous, but sinners to repentance.

Matthew 9:13 KJV

But don't be afraid of those who threaten you. For the time is coming when everything that is covered will be revealed, and all that is secret will be made known to all.

MATTHEW 10:26 NLT

What is the price of two sparrows—one copper coin? But not a single sparrow can fall to the ground without your Father knowing it.

Matthew 10:29 NLT

Whoever acknowledges me before others, I will also acknowledge before my Father in heaven. But whoever disowns me before others, I will disown before my Father in heaven.

Matthew 10:32–33 NIV

Do not suppose that I have come to bring peace to the earth. I did not come to bring peace, but a sword.

Matthew 10:34 NIV

Anyone who loves their father or mother more than me is not worthy of me; anyone who loves their son or daughter more than me is not worthy of me. Whoever does not take up their cross and follow me is not worthy of me.

Matthew 10:37–38 NIV

Whoever finds their life will lose it, and whoever loses their life for my sake will find it.

Matthew 10:39 NIV

The one who welcomes me welcomes him who sent me.

Matthew 10:40 CSB

Anyone who welcomes a prophet because he is a prophet will receive a prophet's reward. And anyone who welcomes a righteous person because he's righteous will receive a righteous person's reward.

Matthew 10:41 CSB

And whoever gives one of these little ones only a cup of cold water in the name of a disciple, assuredly, I say to you, he shall by no means lose his reward.

Matthew 10:42 NKJV

And blessed is the one who isn't offended by me.

Matthew 11:6 CSB

Truly I say to you, among those born of women there has not arisen anyone greater than John the Baptist! Yet the one who is least in the kingdom of heaven is greater than he.

Matthew 11:11 NASB

All things have been committed to me by my Father. No one knows the Son except the Father, and no one knows the Father except the Son and those to whom the Son chooses to reveal him.

Matthew 11:27 NIV

Come to Me, all who are weary and heavy-laden, and I will give you rest. Take My yoke upon you and learn from Me, for I am gentle and humble in heart, and YOU WILL FIND REST FOR YOUR SOULS. For My yoke is easy and My burden is light.

Matthew 11:28–30 NASB

For the Son of man is Lord even of the sabbath day.

Matthew 12:8 KJV

Every kingdom divided against itself will be ruined, and every city or household divided against itself will not stand.

Matthew 12:25 NIV

For whosoever shall do the will of my Father which is in heaven, the same is my brother, and sister, and mother.

Matthew 12:50 KJV

Whoever has will be given more, and they will have an abundance. Whoever does not have, even what they have will be taken from them.

Matthew 13:12 NIV

So listen to the parable of the sower: . . . But the one sown on the good ground—this is one who hears and understands the word, who does produce fruit and yields: some a hundred, some sixty, some thirty times what was sown.

Matthew 13:18, 23 CSB

The one who sows the good seed is the Son of Man; the field is the world; and the good seed—these are the children of the kingdom. The weeds are the children of the evil one, and the enemy who sowed them is the devil. The harvest is the end of the age, and the harvesters are angels.

Matthew 13:37–39 CSB

A prophet is not without honor except in his hometown and in his own household.

Matthew 13:57 NASB

Whoever wants to be my disciple must deny themselves and take up their cross and follow me. For whoever wants to save their life will lose it, but whoever loses their life for me will find it.

Matthew 16:24–25 NIV

For the Son of Man is going to come in his Father's glory with his angels, and then he will reward each person according to what they have done.

Matthew 16:27 NIV

Therefore, whoever humbles himself like this child—this one is the greatest in the kingdom of heaven.

Matthew 18:4 CSB

And whoever welcomes one child like this in my name welcomes me. But whoever causes one of these little ones who believe in me to fall away—it would be better for him if a heavy millstone were hung around his neck and he were drowned in the depths of the sea.

Matthew 18:5–6 CSB

If a man has a hundred sheep and one of them wanders away, what will he do? Won't he leave the ninety-nine others on the hills and go out to search for the one that is lost? And if he finds it, I tell you the truth, he will rejoice over it more than over the ninety-nine that didn't wander away! In the same way, it is not my heavenly Father's will that even one of these little ones should perish.

Matthew 18:12–14 NLT

For where two or three are gathered together in my name, there am I in the midst of them.

Matthew 18:20 KJV

Let the little children come to me, and do not hinder them, for the kingdom of heaven belongs to such as these.

Matthew 19:14 NIV

Truly I tell you, it will be hard for a rich person to enter the kingdom of heaven. Again I tell you, it is easier for a camel to go through the eye of a needle than for a rich person to enter the kingdom of God.

Matthew 19:23–24 CSB

With God all things are possible.

Matthew 19:26 KJV

And everyone who has left houses or brothers or sisters or father or mother or children or fields because of my name will receive a hundred times more and will inherit eternal life.

Matthew 19:29 CSB

But many that are first shall be last; and the last shall be first.

Matthew 19:30 KJV

So the last shall be first, and the first last: for many be called, but few chosen.

Matthew 20:16 KJV

The Son of Man did not come to be served, but to serve, and to give His life a ransom for many.

Matthew 20:28 NASB

For many are called, but few are chosen.

Matthew 22:14 KJV

For in the resurrection they neither marry, nor are given in marriage, but are as the angels of God in heaven.

Matthew 22:30 KJV

Whoever exalts himself shall be humbled; and whoever humbles himself shall be exalted.

Matthew 23:12 NASB

But the one who endures to the end will be saved.

Matthew 24:13 CSB

In fact, unless that time of calamity is shortened, not a single person will survive. But it will be shortened for the sake of God's chosen ones.

Matthew 24:22 NLT

And he will send out his angels with the mighty blast of a trumpet, and they will gather his chosen ones from all over the world—from the farthest ends of the earth and heaven.

Matthew 24:31 NLT

Heaven and earth shall pass away, but my words shall not pass away.

MATTHEW 24:35 KJV

However, no one knows the day or hour when these things will happen, not even the angels in heaven or the Son himself. Only the Father knows.

Matthew 24:36 NLT

A faithful, sensible servant is one to whom the master can give the responsibility of managing his other household servants and feeding them. If the master returns and finds that the servant has done a good job, there will be a reward.

Matthew 24:45–46 NLT

For whoever has will be given more, and they will have an abundance. Whoever does not have, even what they have will be taken from them.

Matthew 25:29 NIV

But when the Son of Man comes in his glory, and all the angels with him, then he will sit upon his glorious throne. All the nations will be gathered in his presence, and he will separate the people as a shepherd separates the sheep from the goats. He will place the sheep at his right hand and the goats at his left.

Matthew 25:31–33 NLT

For this is My blood of the covenant, which is poured out for many for forgiveness of sins.

Matthew 26:28 NASB

All those who take up the sword shall perish by the sword.

Matthew 26:52 NASB

But I want you to know that the Son of Man has authority on earth to forgive sins.

Mark 2:10 NIV

So then, the Son of Man is Lord even of the Sabbath.

Mark 2:28 CSB

I tell you the truth, all sin and blasphemy can be forgiven, but anyone who blasphemes the Holy Spirit will never be forgiven. This is a sin with eternal consequences.

Mark 3:28–29 NLT

Anyone who does God's will is my brother and sister and mother.

Mark 3:35 NLT

For there is nothing hidden that will not be revealed, and nothing concealed that will not be brought to light.

Mark 4:22 CSB

Whoever has will be given more; whoever does not have, even what they have will be taken from them.

Mark 4:25 NIV

A prophet is not without honor except in his hometown and among his own relatives and in his own household.

Mark 6:4 NASB

There is nothing that enters a man from outside which can defile him; but the things which come out of him, those are the things that defile a man.

Mark 7:15 NKJV

Whoever wants to be my disciple must deny themselves and take up their cross and follow me. For whoever wants to save their life will lose it, but whoever loses their life for me and for the gospel will save it.

MARK 8:34–35 NIV

Everything is possible for the one who believes.

Mark 9:23 CSB

If anyone wants to be first, he shall be last of all and servant of all.

Mark 9:35 NASB

Whoever receives one child like this in My name receives Me.

Mark 9:37 NASB

Whoever receives Me does not receive Me, but Him who sent Me.

Mark 9:37 NASB

No one who performs a miracle in my name will soon be able to speak evil of me.

Mark 9:39 NLT

For whoever is not against us is for us.

Mark 9:40 CSB

Whoever causes one of these little ones who believe to stumble, it would be better for him if, with a heavy millstone hung around his neck, he had been cast into the sea.

Mark 9:42 NASB

Whoever divorces his wife and marries another commits adultery against her.

Mark 10:11 CSB

If a woman divorces her husband and marries someone else, she commits adultery.

Mark 10:12 NLT

Truly I tell you, whoever does not receive the kingdom of God like a little child will never enter it.

Mark 10:15 CSB

How hard it will be for those who are wealthy to enter the kingdom of God! . . . . Children, how hard it is to enter the kingdom of God! It is easier for a camel to go through the eye of a needle than for a rich man to enter the kingdom of God. . . . With people it is impossible, but not with God.

Mark 10:23–25, 27 NASB

With God all things are possible.

Mark 10:27 KJV

No one who has left home or brothers or sisters or mother or father or children or fields for me and the gospel will fail to receive a hundred times as much in this present age: homes, brothers, sisters, mothers, children and fields—along with persecutions—and in the age to come eternal life.

Mark 10:29–30 NIV

But many who are first will be last, and the last first.

Mark 10:31 NIV

For even the Son of Man did not come to be served, but to serve, and to give his life as a ransom for many.

Mark 10:45 CSB

Truly I tell you, if anyone says to this mountain, "Go, throw yourself into the sea," and does not doubt in their heart but believes that what they say will happen, it will be done for them.

Mark 11:23 NIV

For when the dead rise, they will neither marry nor be given in marriage. In this respect they will be like the angels in heaven.

Mark 12:25 NLT

He is not the God of the dead, but the God of the living.

Mark 12:27 KJV

If the Lord had not cut short those days, no one would survive. But for the sake of the elect, whom he has chosen, he has shortened them.

Mark 13:20 NIV

At that time people will see the Son of Man coming in clouds with great power and glory. And he will send his angels and gather his elect from the four winds, from the ends of the earth to the ends of the heavens.

Mark 13:26–27 NIV

Heaven and earth shall pass away: but my words shall not pass away.

Mark 13:31 KJV

Whoever believes and is baptized will be saved,
but whoever does not believe will be condemned.

Mark 16:16 CSB

But I want you to know that the Son of Man has
authority on earth to forgive sins.

Luke 5:24 NIV

I have not come to call the righteous but sinners
to repentance.

Luke 5:32 NASB

A good person produces good out of the good stored up in his heart.

Luke 6:45 CSB

I will show you what someone is like who comes to me, hears my words, and acts on them: He is like a man building a house, who dug deep and laid the foundation on the rock. When the flood came, the river crashed against that house and couldn't shake it, because it was well built.

Luke 6:47–48 CSB

But anyone who hears and doesn't obey is like a person who builds a house right on the ground, without a foundation. When the floods sweep down against that house, it will collapse into a heap of ruins.

Luke 6:49 NLT

Blessed is anyone who does not stumble on account of me.

Luke 7:23 NIV

Whoever has been forgiven little loves little.

Luke 7:47 NIV

And the seeds that fell on the good soil represent honest, good-hearted people who hear God's word, cling to it, and patiently produce a huge harvest.

Luke 8:15 NLT

For nothing is concealed that won't be revealed, and nothing hidden that won't be made known and brought to light.

Luke 8:17 CSB

Whoever has, more will be given to him; and whoever does not have, even what he thinks he has will be taken away from him.

Luke 8:18 CSB

My mother and my brothers are all those who hear God's word and obey it.

Luke 8:21 NLT

Ask and it will be given to you; seek and you will find; knock and the door will be opened to you.

Luke 11:9 NIV

Whoever wants to be my disciple must deny themselves and take up their cross daily and follow me.

Luke 9:23 NIV

For whoever wants to save their life will lose it, but whoever loses their life for me will save it.

Luke 9:24 NIV

Whoever is ashamed of me and my words, the Son of Man will be ashamed of them when he comes in his glory and in the glory of the Father and of the holy angels.

Luke 9:26 NIV

Anyone who welcomes a little child like this on my behalf welcomes me.

Luke 9:48 NLT

Anyone who welcomes me also welcomes my Father who sent me.

Luke 9:48 NLT

For whoever is least among you—this one is great.

Luke 9:48 CSB

No one who puts his hand to the plow and looks back is fit for the kingdom of God.

Luke 9:62 CSB

For everyone who asks receives, and the one who seeks finds, and to the one who knocks, the door will be opened.

Luke 11:10 CSB

If you then, who are evil, know how to give good gifts to your children, how much more will the heavenly Father give the Holy Spirit to those who ask him?

Luke 11:13 CSB

Whoever is not with me is against me, and whoever does not gather with me scatters.

Luke 11:23 ESV

Blessed are those who hear the word of God and keep it!

LUKE 11:28 NKJV

I tell you the truth, everyone who acknowledges me publicly here on earth, the Son of Man will also acknowledge in the presence of God's angels.

Luke 12:8 NLT

But anyone who denies me here on earth will be denied before God's angels.

Luke 12:9 NLT

Anyone who speaks against the Son of Man can be forgiven, but anyone who blasphemes the Holy Spirit will not be forgiven.

Luke 12:10 NLT

Do not be afraid, little flock, for your Father has been pleased to give you the kingdom.

Luke 12:32 NIV

It will be good for those servants whose master finds them watching when he comes. Truly I tell you, he will dress himself to serve, will have them recline at the table and will come and wait on them. It will be good for those servants whose master finds them ready, even if he comes in the middle of the night or toward daybreak.

Luke 12:37–38 NIV

A faithful, sensible servant is one to whom the master can give the responsibility of managing his other household servants and feeding them. If the master returns and finds that the servant has done a good job, there will be a reward. I tell you the truth, the master will put that servant in charge of all he owns.

Luke 12:42–44 NLT

For everyone who exalts himself will be humbled, and he who humbles himself will be exalted.

Luke 14:11 NASB

There will be more joy in heaven over one sinner who repents than over ninety-nine righteous people who don't need repentance.

Luke 15:7 CSB

There is joy in the presence of God's angels over one sinner who repents.

Luke 15:10 CSB

Whoever can be trusted with very little can also be trusted with much, and whoever is dishonest with very little will also be dishonest with much.

Luke 16:10 NIV

No servant can serve two masters, since either he will hate one and love the other, or he will be devoted to one and despise the other. You cannot serve both God and money.

Luke 16:13 CSB

But it is easier for heaven and earth to pass away than for one dot of the Law to become void.

Luke 16:17 ESV

When the Son of Man comes again, he will shine like lightning, which flashes across the sky and lights it up from one side to the other.

Luke 17:24 NCV

Whoever seeks to keep his life will lose it, and whoever loses his life will preserve it.

Luke 17:33 NASB

Now, will not God bring about justice for His elect who cry to Him day and night, and will He delay long over them? I tell you that He will bring about justice for them quickly.

Luke 18:7–8 NASB

For all those who exalt themselves will be humbled, and those who humble themselves will be exalted.

Luke 18:14 NIV

Truly I tell you, whoever does not receive the kingdom of God like a little child will never enter it.

Luke 18:17 CSB

How hard it is for those who are wealthy to enter the kingdom of God! For it is easier for a camel to go through the eye of a needle than for a rich man to enter the kingdom of God.

**LUKE 18:24–25** NASB

The things that are impossible with people are possible with God.

Luke 18:27 NASB

Truly I say to you, there is no one who has left house or wife or brothers or parents or children, for the sake of the kingdom of God, who will not receive many times as much at this time and in the age to come, eternal life.

Luke 18:29–30 NASB

For the Son of man is come to seek and to save that which was lost.

Luke 19:10 KJV

I tell you that to everyone who has, more shall be given, but from the one who does not have, even what he does have shall be taken away.

Luke 19:26 NASB

"The stone that the builders rejected has now become the cornerstone." Everyone who stumbles over that stone will be broken to pieces, and it will crush anyone it falls on.

Luke 20:17–18 NLT

There will be signs in sun and moon and stars, and on the earth dismay among nations, in perplexity at the roaring of the sea and the waves, men fainting from fear and the expectation of the things which are coming upon the world; for the powers of the heavens will be shaken. Then they will see THE SON OF MAN COMING IN A CLOUD with power and great glory.

Luke 21:25–27 NASB

Heaven and earth shall pass away: but my words shall not pass away.

Luke 21:33 KJV

For that day will come upon everyone living on the earth.

Luke 21:35 NLT

But from now on, the Son of Man will be seated at the right hand of the power of God.

Luke 22:69 CSB

Very truly I tell you, no one can see the kingdom of God unless they are born again.

John 3:3 NIV

Very truly I tell you, no one can enter the kingdom of God unless they are born of water and the Spirit.

John 3:5 NIV

Just as Moses lifted up the snake in the wilderness, so the Son of Man must be lifted up, so that everyone who believes in him may have eternal life.

John 3:14–15 CSB

For God so loved the world that he gave his one and only Son, that whoever believes in him shall not perish but have eternal life. For God did not send his Son into the world to condemn the world, but to save the world through him. Whoever believes in him is not condemned, but whoever does not believe stands condemned already because they have not believed in the name of God's one and only Son.

JOHN 3:16–18 NIV

Those who drink the water I give will never be thirsty again. It becomes a fresh, bubbling spring within them, giving them eternal life.

John 4:14 NLT

The time is coming—indeed it's here now—when true worshipers will worship the Father in spirit and in truth.

John 4:23 NLT

Just as the Father raises the dead and gives them life, so the Son also gives life to whom he wants.

John 5:21 CSB

Truly I tell you, anyone who hears my word and believes him who sent me has eternal life and will not come under judgment but has passed from death to life.

John 5:24 CSB

Truly I tell you, an hour is coming, and is now here, when the dead will hear the voice of the Son of God, and those who hear will live. For just as the Father has life in himself, so also he has granted to the Son to have life in himself. And he has granted him the right to pass judgment, because he is the Son of Man.

John 5:25–27 CSB

Don't be so surprised! Indeed, the time is coming when all the dead in their graves will hear the voice of God's Son, and they will rise again. Those who have done good will rise to experience eternal life, and those who have continued in evil will rise to experience judgment.

John 5:28–29 NLT

I am the bread of life. Whoever comes to me will never go hungry, and whoever believes in me will never be thirsty.

John 6:35 NIV

All that the Father gives Me will come to Me, and the one who comes to Me I will certainly not cast out.

John 6:37 NASB

This is the will of him who sent me: that I should lose none of those he has given me but should raise them up on the last day. For this is the will of my Father: that everyone who sees the Son and believes in him will have eternal life, and I will raise him up on the last day.

JOHN 6:39–40 CSB

For no one can come to me unless the Father who sent me draws them to me, and at the last day I will raise them up.

John 6:44 NLT

Truly I tell you, anyone who believes has eternal life.

John 6:47 CSB

I am the bread of life. . . . This is the bread that comes down from heaven so that anyone may eat of it and not die. I am the living bread that came down from heaven. If anyone eats of this bread he will live forever. The bread that I will give for the life of the world is my flesh.

John 6:48, 50–51 CSB

The one who eats my flesh and drinks my blood has eternal life, and I will raise him up on the last day, because my flesh is true food and my blood is true drink. The one who eats my flesh and drinks my blood remains in me, and I in him. Just as the living Father sent me and I live because of the Father, so the one who feeds on me will live because of me. . . . The one who eats this bread will live forever.

John 6:54–57, 58 CSB

No one can come to me unless the Father has enabled them.

John 6:65 NIV

Anyone who chooses to do the will of God will find out whether my teaching comes from God or whether I speak on my own.

John 7:17 NIV

Let anyone who is thirsty come to me and drink. Whoever believes in me, as Scripture has said, rivers of living water will flow from within them.

John 7:37–38 NIV

I am the light of the world. Anyone who follows me will never walk in the darkness but will have the light of life.

John 8:12 CSB

Truly, truly, I say to you, everyone who commits sin is the slave of sin.

John 8:34 NASB

He who is of God hears the words of God.

John 8:47 NASB

Very truly I tell you, whoever obeys my word will never see death.

John 8:51 NIV

Yes, I am the gate. Those who come in through me will be saved. They will come and go freely and will find good pastures.

John 10:9 NLT

I am the good shepherd; I know my own sheep, and they know me, just as my Father knows me and I know the Father. So I sacrifice my life for the sheep. I have other sheep, too, that are not in this sheepfold. I must bring them also. They will listen to my voice, and there will be one flock with one shepherd.

John 10:14–16 NLT

My sheep listen to my voice; I know them, and they follow me. I give them eternal life, and they will never perish. No one can snatch them away from me, for my Father has given them to me, and he is more powerful than anyone else. No one can snatch them from the Father's hand.

JOHN 10:27–29 NLT

I am the resurrection and the life. Anyone who believes in me will live, even after dying. Everyone who lives in me and believes in me will never ever die.

John 11:25–26 NLT

Anyone who loves their life will lose it, while anyone who hates their life in this world will keep it for eternal life.

John 12:25 NIV

Whoever serves me must follow me; and where I am, my servant also will be. My Father will honor the one who serves me.

John 12:26 NIV

And I, when I am lifted up from the earth, will draw all people to myself.

John 12:32 NIV

The one who believes in me believes not in me, but in him who sent me. And the one who sees me sees him who sent me.

John 12:44–45 CSB

I have come as light into the world, so that everyone who believes in me would not remain in darkness.

John 12:46 CSB

Truly, truly, I say to you, he who receives whomever I send receives Me; and he who receives Me receives Him who sent Me.

John 13:20 NASB

I am the way, and the truth, and the life; no one comes to the Father but through Me.

John 14:6 NASB

Anyone who has seen me has seen the Father.

John 14:9 NIV

Very truly I tell you, whoever believes in me will do the works I have been doing, and they will do even greater things than these, because I am going to the Father.

John 14:12 NIV

Those who accept my commandments and obey them are the ones who love me. And because they love me, my Father will love them. And I will love them and reveal myself to each of them.

John 14:21 NLT

Anyone who loves me will obey my teaching. My Father will love them, and we will come to them and make our home with them. Anyone who does not love me will not obey my teaching. These words you hear are not my own; they belong to the Father who sent me.

John 14:23–24 NIV

I am the true vine, and My Father is the vine-dresser. Every branch in Me that does not bear fruit, He takes away; and every branch that bears fruit, He prunes it so that it may bear more fruit.

John 15:1–2 NASB

As the Father has loved me, so have I loved you. Now remain in my love. If you keep my commands, you will remain in my love, just as I have kept my Father's commands and remain in his love.

JOHN 15:9–10 NIV

And when [the Holy Spirit] comes, he will convict the world concerning sin and righteousness and judgment: concerning sin, because they do not believe in me; concerning righteousness, because I go to the Father, and you will see me no longer; concerning judgment, because the ruler of this world is judged.

John 16:8–11 ESV

You gave him authority over all people, so that he may give eternal life to everyone you have given him. This is eternal life: that they may know you, the only true God, and the one you have sent—Jesus Christ.

John 17:2–3 CSB

I pray not only for these, but also for those who believe in me through their word. May they all be one, as you, Father, are in me and I am in you. May they also be in us, so that the world may believe you sent me. I have given them the glory you have given me, so that they may be one as we are one. I am in them and you are in me, so that they may be made completely one, that the world may know you have sent me and have loved them as you have loved me.

John 17:20–23 CSB

Father, I want those you have given me to be with me where I am, so that they will see my glory, which you have given me because you loved me before the world's foundation.

John 17:24 CSB

Blessed are those who believe without seeing me.

John 20:29 NLT

To the one who is victorious, I will give the right to eat from the tree of life, which is in the paradise of God.

Revelation 2:7 NIV

The one who is victorious will not be hurt at all by the second death.

Revelation 2:11 NIV

To the one who is victorious, I will give some of the hidden manna. I will also give that person a white stone with a new name written on it, known only to the one who receives it.

Revelation 2:17 NIV

To all who are victorious, who obey me to the very end, to them I will give authority over all the nations. They will rule the nations with an iron rod and smash them like clay pots. They will have the same authority I received from my Father, and I will also give them the morning star!

Revelation 2:26–28 NLT

The one who is victorious will, like them, be dressed in white. I will never blot out the name of that person from the book of life, but will acknowledge that name before my Father and his angels.

Revelation 3:5 NIV

All who are victorious will become pillars in the Temple of my God, and they will never have to leave it. And I will write on them the name of my God, and they will be citizens in the city of my God—the new Jerusalem that comes down from heaven from my God. And I will also write on them my new name.

Revelation 3:12 NLT

As many as I love, I rebuke and chasten: be zealous therefore, and repent.

Revelation 3:19 KJV

Behold, I stand at the door and knock; if anyone hears My voice and opens the door, I will come in to him and will dine with him, and he with Me.

REVELATION 3:20 NASB

To the one who conquers I will give the right to sit with me on my throne, just as I also conquered and sat down with my Father on his throne.

Revelation 3:21 CSB

Look, I will come as unexpectedly as a thief! Blessed are all who are watching for me, who keep their clothing ready so they will not have to walk around naked and ashamed.

Revelation 16:15 NLT

Behold, I am making all things new.

Revelation 21:5 NASB

To the thirsty I will give water without cost from the spring of the water of life.

Revelation 21:6 NIV

All who are victorious will inherit all these blessings, and I will be their God, and they will be my children.

Revelation 21:7 NLT

Look, I am coming soon! Blessed is the one who keeps the words of the prophecy of this book.

Revelation 22:7 csb

Look, I am coming soon, bringing my reward with me to repay all people according to their deeds.

Revelation 22:12 nlt

Blessed are those who wash their robes, so that they may have the right to the tree of life and may enter the city by the gates.

Revelation 22:14 CSB

Yes, I am coming soon.

Revelation 22:20 NIV

# PART 2

# WHAT JESUS PROMISED THE TWELVE DISCIPLES

## (WHICH MAY OR MAY NOT BE FOR EVERYBODY)

Follow me, and I will make you fishers of men.

Matthew 4:19 KJV

Blessed are you when others revile you and persecute you and utter all kinds of evil against you falsely on my account. Rejoice and be glad, for your reward is great in heaven, for so they persecuted the prophets who were before you.

Matthew 5:11–12 ESV

You are the salt of the earth.

Matthew 5:13 NKJV

You are the light of the world.

Matthew 5:14 NKJV

Beware of practicing your righteousness before other people in order to be seen by them, for then you will have no reward from your Father who is in heaven. Thus, when you give to the needy, sound no trumpet before you, as the hypocrites do in the synagogues and in the streets, that they may be praised by others. Truly, I say to you, they have received their reward. But when you give to the needy, do not let your left hand know what your right hand is doing, so that your giving may be in secret. And your Father who sees in secret will reward you.

Matthew 6:1–4 ESV

When you pray, go into your room and shut the door and pray to your Father who is in secret. And your Father who sees in secret will reward you.

Matthew 6:6 ESV

Your Father knows what you need before you ask him.

Matthew 6:8 ESV

If you forgive other people when they sin against you, your heavenly Father will also forgive you.

Matthew 6:14 NIV

When you fast, put oil on your head and wash your face, so that your fasting isn't obvious to others but to your Father who is in secret. And your Father who sees in secret will reward you.

MATTHEW 6:17–18 CSB

Store up for yourselves treasures in heaven, where neither moth nor rust destroys, and where thieves don't break in and steal.

Matthew 6:20 CSB

The eye is the lamp of the body. If your eyes are healthy, your whole body will be full of light. But if your eyes are unhealthy, your whole body will be full of darkness.

Matthew 6:22–23 NIV

But if God so clothes the grass of the field, which today is alive and tomorrow is thrown into the oven, will he not much more clothe you, O you of little faith? Therefore do not be anxious, saying, "What shall we eat?" or "What shall we drink?" or "What shall we wear?" For the Gentiles seek after all these things, and your heavenly Father knows that you need them all. But seek first the kingdom of God and his righteousness, and all these things will be added to you.

Matthew 6:30–33 ESV

Ask, and it will be given to you; seek, and you will find; knock, and it will be opened to you.

Matthew 7:7 NKJV

When they deliver you up, do not worry about how or what you should speak. For it will be given to you in that hour what you should speak; for it is not you who speak, but the Spirit of your Father who speaks in you.

Matthew 10:19–20 NKJV

Brother will deliver brother over to death, and the father his child, and children will rise against parents and have them put to death, and you will be hated by all for my name's sake. But the one who endures to the end will be saved. When they persecute you in one town, flee to the next, for truly, I say to you, you will not have gone through all the towns of Israel before the Son of Man comes.

Matthew 10:21–23 ESV

Even the hairs of your head are all numbered.

Matthew 10:30 ESV

You are of more value than many sparrows.

Matthew 10:31 ESV

Whoever receives you receives me.

Matthew 10:40 ESV

Blessed are you, Simon Bar-Jonah, for flesh and blood has not revealed this to you, but My Father who is in heaven. And I also say to you that you are Peter, and on this rock I will build My church, and the gates of Hades shall not prevail against it. And I will give you the keys of the kingdom of heaven, and whatever you bind on earth will be bound in heaven, and whatever you loose on earth will be loosed in heaven.

Matthew 16:17–19 NKJV

And I tell you the truth, some standing here right now will not die before they see the Son of Man coming in his Kingdom.

Matthew 16:28 NLT

Truly I tell you, if you have faith as small as a mustard seed, you can say to this mountain, "Move from here to there," and it will move. Nothing will be impossible for you.

Matthew 17:20 NIV

The Son of Man is about to be betrayed into the hands of men. They will kill him, and on the third day he will be raised up.

Matthew 17:22–23 CSB

Truly, I say to you, whatever you bind on earth shall be bound in heaven, and whatever you loose on earth shall be loosed in heaven.

Matthew 18:18 ESV

Again I say to you, if two of you agree on earth about anything they ask, it will be done for them by my Father in heaven.

Matthew 18:19 ESV

Assuredly I say to you, that in the regeneration, when the Son of Man sits on the throne of His glory, you who have followed Me will also sit on twelve thrones, judging the twelve tribes of Israel.

Matthew 19:28 NKJV

See, we are going up to Jerusalem. The Son of Man will be handed over to the chief priests and scribes, and they will condemn him to death. They will hand him over to the Gentiles to be mocked, flogged, and crucified, and on the third day he will be raised.

Matthew 20:18–19 csb

Whoever would be great among you must be your servant, and whoever would be first among you must be your slave.

Matthew 20:26–27 esv

Truly I tell you, if you have faith and do not doubt, not only can you do what was done to the fig tree, but also you can say to this mountain, "Go, throw yourself into the sea," and it will be done. If you believe, you will receive whatever you ask for in prayer.

Matthew 21:21–22 NIV

Do you see all these buildings? I tell you the truth, they will be completely demolished. Not one stone will be left on top of another!

Matthew 24:2 NLT

You know that after two days is the Passover, and the Son of Man will be delivered up to be crucified.

Matthew 26:2 NKJV

You will always have the poor with you, but you will not always have me.

Matthew 26:11 NCV

Truly, I say to you, wherever this gospel is proclaimed in the whole world, what she has done will also be told in memory of her.

Matthew 26:13 ESV

Mark my words—I will not drink wine again until the day I drink it new with you in my Father's Kingdom.

Matthew 26:29 NLT

This very night you will all fall away on account of me, for it is written: "I will strike the shepherd, and the sheep of the flock will be scattered." But after I have risen, I will go ahead of you into Galilee.

Matthew 26:31–32 NIV

I am with you always, even unto the end of the world.

MATTHEW 28:20 KJV

Follow Me, and I will make you become fishers of men.

Mark 1:17 NKJV

To you it has been given to know the mystery of the kingdom of God; but to those who are outside, all things come in parables, so that "Seeing they may see and not perceive, and hearing they may hear and not understand; lest they should turn, and their sins be forgiven them."

Mark 4:11–12 NKJV

Take care what you listen to. By your standard of measure it will be measured to you; and more will be given you besides.

Mark 4:24 NASB

Truly, I say to you, there are some standing here who will not taste death until they see the kingdom of God after it has come with power.

Mark 9:1 ESV

The Son of Man is to be delivered into the hands of men, and they will kill Him; and when He has been killed, He will rise three days later.

Mark 9:31 NASB

For whoever gives you a cup of water to drink in My name, because you belong to Christ, assuredly, I say to you, he will by no means lose his reward.

Mark 9:41 NKJV

See, we are going up to Jerusalem, and the Son of Man will be delivered over to the chief priests and the scribes, and they will condemn him to death and deliver him over to the Gentiles. And they will mock him and spit on him, and flog him and kill him. And after three days he will rise.

Mark 10:33–34 ESV

Whoever would be first among you must be slave of all.

Mark 10:44 ESV

Therefore I tell you, whatever you ask in prayer, believe that you have received it, and it will be yours.

Mark 11:24 ESV

Whenever you stand praying, if you have anything against anyone, forgive him, that your Father in heaven may also forgive you your trespasses.

Mark 11:25 NKJV

Do you see these great buildings? Not one stone will be left upon another—all will be thrown down.

Mark 13:2 CSB

Learn this lesson from the fig tree: As soon as its branch becomes tender and sprouts leaves, you know that summer is near. In the same way, when you see these things happening, recognize that he is near—at the door. Truly I tell you, this generation will certainly not pass away until all these things take place.

Mark 13:28–30 CSB

Now concerning that day or hour no one knows—neither the angels in heaven nor the Son—but only the Father. Watch! Be alert! For you don't know when the time is coming.

Mark 13:32–33 CSB

But after I am raised up, I will go before you to Galilee.

Mark 14:28 ESV

From now on you will catch men.

Luke 5:10 NKJV

Blessed are you who are poor, for yours is the kingdom of God.

Luke 6:20 ESV

Blessed are you who are hungry now, for you shall be satisfied.

Luke 6:21 ESV

Blessed are you who weep now, for you shall laugh.

Luke 6:21 ESV

Blessed are you when people hate you and when they exclude you and revile you and spurn your name as evil, on account of the Son of Man! Rejoice in that day, and leap for joy, for behold, your reward is great in heaven.

Luke 6:22–23 ESV

But love your enemies, and do good, and lend, expecting nothing in return, and your reward will be great, and you will be sons of the Most High, for he is kind to the ungrateful and the evil.

Luke 6:35 ESV

Judge not, and you will not be judged; condemn not, and you will not be condemned.

Luke 6:37 ESV

Forgive, and you will be forgiven.

Luke 6:37 ESV

Give, and it will be given to you. Good measure, pressed down, shaken together, running over, will be put into your lap. For with the measure you use it will be measured back to you.

Luke 6:38 ESV

It is necessary that the Son of Man suffer many things and be rejected by the elders, chief priests, and scribes, be killed, and be raised the third day.

Luke 9:22 CSB

Truly I tell you, some who are standing here will not taste death before they see the kingdom of God.

Luke 9:27 NIV

Let these words sink into your ears; for the Son of Man is going to be delivered into the hands of men.

Luke 9:44 NASB

The one who listens to you listens to Me, and the one who rejects you rejects Me.

Luke 10:16 NASB

Behold, I have given you authority to tread on serpents and scorpions, and over all the power of the enemy, and nothing will injure you.

Luke 10:19 NASB

Your names are written in heaven.

Luke 10:20 KJV

Blessed are the eyes which see the things you see.

Luke 10:23 NASB

So I say to you, ask, and it will be given to you; seek, and you will find; knock, and it will be opened to you.

Luke 11:9 NKJV

Indeed, the very hairs of your head are all numbered. Do not fear; you are more valuable than many sparrows.

Luke 12:7 NASB

Whenever they bring you before synagogues and rulers and authorities, don't worry about how you should defend yourselves or what you should say. For the Holy Spirit will teach you at that very hour what must be said.

Luke 12:11–12 CSB

Consider the ravens: They do not sow or reap, they have no storeroom or barn; yet God feeds them. And how much more valuable you are than birds!

Luke 12:24 NIV

Look at the lilies and how they grow. They don't work or make their clothing, yet Solomon in all his glory was not dressed as beautifully as they are. And if God cares so wonderfully for flowers that are here today and thrown into the fire tomorrow, he will certainly care for you.

Luke 12:27–28 NLT

But seek his kingdom, and these things will be provided for you.

Luke 12:31 CSB

Fear not, little flock; for it is your Father's good pleasure to give you the kingdom.

Luke 12:32 KJV

The Son of Man is coming at an hour that you do not expect.

Luke 12:40 NASB

Do you think I came to bring peace on earth? No, I tell you, but division.

Luke 12:51 NIV

I tell you, use worldly wealth to gain friends for yourselves, so that when it is gone, you will be welcomed into eternal dwellings.

Luke 16:9 NIV

If you have faith as small as a mustard seed, you can say to this mulberry tree, "Be uprooted and planted in the sea," and it will obey you.

LUKE 17:6 NIV

He must suffer many things and be rejected by the people of this time.

Luke 17:25 NCV

Listen, we're going up to Jerusalem, where all the predictions of the prophets concerning the Son of Man will come true. He will be handed over to the Romans, and he will be mocked, treated shamefully, and spit upon. They will flog him with a whip and kill him, but on the third day he will rise again.

Luke 18:31–33 NLT

And everyone will hate you because you are my followers. But not a hair of your head will perish! By standing firm, you will win your souls.

Luke 21:17–19 NLT

So when all these things begin to happen, stand and look up, for your salvation is near.

Luke 21:28 NLT

I tell you the truth, this generation will not pass from the scene until all these things have taken place.

Luke 21:32 NLT

Simon, Simon, Satan has asked to sift all of you as wheat. But I have prayed for you, Simon, that your faith may not fail. And when you have turned back, strengthen your brothers. . . . I tell you, Peter, before the rooster crows today, you will deny three times that you know me.

Luke 22:31–32, 34 NIV

I will send the Holy Spirit, just as my Father promised. But stay here in the city until the Holy Spirit comes and fills you with power from heaven.

Luke 24:49 NLT

Because I said to you, "I saw you under the fig tree," do you believe? You will see greater things than these. . . . Most assuredly, I say to you, hereafter you shall see heaven open, and the angels of God ascending and descending upon the Son of Man.

John 1:50–51 NKJV

The words that I have spoken to you are spirit and are life.

JOHN 6:63 NASB

As long as I am in the world, I am the light of the world.

John 9:5 KJV

For the poor you have with you always, but Me you do not have always.

John 12:8 NKJV

You don't understand now what I am doing, but you will understand later.

John 13:7 NCV

Truly I tell you, a servant is not greater than his master, and a messenger is not greater than the one who sent him. If you know these things, you are blessed if you do them.

John 13:16–17 CSB

By this everyone will know that you are my disciples, if you love one another.

John 13:35 CSB

Where I go, you [Peter] cannot follow Me now; but you will follow later.

John 13:36 NASB

I tell you the truth, Peter—before the rooster crows tomorrow morning, you will deny three times that you even know me.

John 13:38 NLT

In My Father's house are many mansions; if it were not so, I would have told you. I go to prepare a place for you. And if I go and prepare a place for you, I will come again and receive you to Myself; that where I am, there you may be also.

John 14:2–3 NKJV

If you know me, you will also know my Father. From now on you do know him and have seen him.

John 14:7 CSB

Whatever you ask in My name, that will I do, so that the Father may be glorified in the Son. If you ask Me anything in My name, I will do it.

JOHN 14:13–14 NASB

If you love me, keep my commands. And I will ask the Father, and he will give you another advocate to help you and be with you forever—the Spirit of truth. The world cannot accept him, because it neither sees him nor knows him. But you know him, for he lives with you and will be in you. I will not leave you as orphans; I will come to you.

John 14:15–18 NIV

After a little while the world will no longer see Me, but you will see Me; because I live, you will live also. In that day you will know that I am in My Father, and you in Me, and I in you.

John 14:19–20 NASB

But the Counselor, the Holy Spirit, whom the Father will send in my name, will teach you all things and remind you of everything I have told you.

John 14:26 CSB

Peace I leave with you; my peace I give you.

John 14:27 NIV

You are already clean because of the word which I have spoken to you.

John 15:3 NKJV

Abide in me, and I in you. As the branch cannot bear fruit by itself, unless it abides in the vine, neither can you, unless you abide in me.

John 15:4 ESV

I am the vine; you are the branches. If you remain in me and I in you, you will bear much fruit; apart from me you can do nothing. If you do not remain in me, you are like a branch that is thrown away and withers; such branches are picked up, thrown into the fire and burned.

John 15:5–6 NIV

If you remain in me and my words remain in you, ask whatever you wish, and it will be done for you.

John 15:7 NIV

Everything that I learned from my Father I have made known to you.

John 15:15 NIV

You did not choose me, but I chose you and appointed you that you should go and bear fruit and that your fruit should abide, so that whatever you ask the Father in my name, he may give it to you.

John 15:16 ESV

When the Helper comes, whom I will send to you from the Father, that is the Spirit of truth who proceeds from the Father, He will testify about Me, and you will testify also, because you have been with Me from the beginning.

John 15:26–27 NASB

Nevertheless, I tell you the truth: it is to your advantage that I go away, for if I do not go away, the Helper will not come to you. But if I go, I will send him to you.

John 16:7 ESV

When the Spirit of truth comes, he will guide you into all the truth, for he will not speak on his own authority, but whatever he hears he will speak, and he will declare to you the things that are to come. He will glorify me, for he will take what is mine and declare it to you. All that the Father has is mine; therefore I said that he will take what is mine and declare it to you.

John 16:13–15 ESV

After a little while you will not see me, and then after a little while you will see me again.

John 16:16 NCV

Truly I tell you, you will weep and mourn, but the world will rejoice. You will become sorrowful, but your sorrow will turn to joy.

John 16:20 CSB

Therefore you now have sorrow; but I will see you again and your heart will rejoice, and your joy no one will take from you.

JOHN 16:22 NKJV

Truly, truly, I say to you, whatever you ask of the Father in my name, he will give it to you.

John 16:23 ESV

Ask, and you will receive, that your joy may be full.

John 16:24 NKJV

Though I have been speaking figuratively, a time is coming when I will no longer use this kind of language but will tell you plainly about my Father.

John 16:25 NIV

A time is coming and in fact has come when you will be scattered, each to your own home. You will leave me all alone.

John 16:32 NIV

I have told you these things, so that in me you may have peace. In this world you will have trouble. But take heart! I have overcome the world.

John 16:33 NIV

I speak these things in the world so that they may have my joy completed in them.

John 17:13 CSB

If you forgive the sins of any, they are forgiven them; if you withhold forgiveness from any, it is withheld.

John 20:23 ESV

I tell you the truth, when you [Peter] were young, you were able to do as you liked; you dressed yourself and went wherever you wanted to go. But when you are old, you will stretch out your hands, and others will dress you and take you where you don't want to go.

John 21:18 NLT

Wait here to receive the promise from the Father which I told you about. John baptized people with water, but in a few days you will be baptized with the Holy Spirit.

Acts 1:4–5 NCV

But you will receive power when the Holy Spirit comes on you; and you will be my witnesses in Jerusalem, and in all Judea and Samaria, and to the ends of the earth.

Acts 1:8 NIV

# PART 3

# WHAT JESUS PROMISED OTHERS

*To a paralyzed man*
Take heart, my son; your sins are forgiven.

Matthew 9:2 ESV

*To two blind men*
Because of your faith, it will happen.

Matthew 9:29 NLT

Woe to you, Chorazin! Woe to you, Bethsaida! For if the mighty works done in you had been done in Tyre and Sidon, they would have repented long ago in sackcloth and ashes. But I tell you, it will be more bearable on the day of judgment for Tyre and Sidon than for you.

Matthew 11:21–22 ESV

And you, Capernaum, will you be exalted to heaven? You will be brought down to Hades. For if the mighty works done in you had been done in Sodom, it would have remained until this day. But I tell you that it will be more tolerable on the day of judgment for the land of Sodom than for you.

Matthew 11:23–24 ESV

*To the Pharisees*
For as Jonah was three days and three nights in the belly of the great fish, so will the Son of Man be three days and three nights in the heart of the earth.

Matthew 12:40 NKJV

*To a Canaanite woman*
Woman, you have great faith! I will do what you asked.

Matthew 15:28 NCV

*To a rich young man*
If you want to be perfect, go, sell what you have and give to the poor, and you will have treasure in heaven.

Matthew 19:21 NKJV

*To chief priests and Pharisees*
Therefore I tell you that the kingdom of God will be taken away from you and given to a people who will produce its fruit.

Matthew 21:43 NIV

*To a high priest*
From now on you will see the Son of Man seated at the right hand of Power and coming on the clouds of heaven.

Matthew 26:64 ESV

*To the women who had come to the tomb*
Go and tell my brothers to go to Galilee, and there they will see me.

Matthew 28:10 ESV

*To the people of Galilee*
The time is fulfilled, and the kingdom of God
is at hand.

Mark 1:15 NKJV

*To the Pharisees*
Why does this generation seek for a sign? Truly I
say to you, no sign will be given to this generation.

Mark 8:12 NASB

*To the guests at Simon's house*
For you always have the poor with you, and whenever you want, you can do good for them. But you will not always have me.

Mark 14:7 ESV

*To the guests at Simon's house*
And truly, I say to you, wherever the gospel is proclaimed in the whole world, what she has done will be told in memory of her.

Mark 14:9 ESV

*To a high priest*
You will see the Son of Man seated in the place of power at God's right hand and coming on the clouds of heaven.

Mark 14:62 NLT

*To the woman who anointed his feet with her tears*
Your sins are forgiven. . . . Your faith has saved you; go in peace."

Luke 7:48, 50 ESV

*To Jairus, whose daughter Jesus healed*
Don't be afraid; just believe, and she will be healed.

Luke 8:50 NIV

*To a crowd of listeners*

If you are filled with light, with no dark corners, then your whole life will be radiant, as though a floodlight were filling you with light.

LUKE 11:36 NLT

*To a Pharisee*
So clean the inside by giving gifts to the poor, and you will be clean all over.

Luke 11:41 NLT

*To a person who asked Jesus a question*
People will come from east and west and north and south, and will take their places at the feast in the kingdom of God.

Luke 13:29 NIV

*To a person who asked Jesus a question*
There are those who are last now who will be first in the future. And there are those who are first now who will be last in the future.

Luke 13:30 NCV

*To a Pharisee who was hosting a meal for Jesus*
On the contrary, when you host a banquet, invite those who are poor, maimed, lame, or blind. And you will be blessed, because they cannot repay you; for you will be repaid at the resurrection of the righteous.

Luke 14:13–14 CSB

*To a large crowd traveling with Jesus*
And if you do not carry your own cross and follow
me, you cannot be my disciple.

Luke 14:27 NLT

*To a blind beggar*
Receive your sight; your faith has made you well.

Luke 18:42 NKJV

*To Zacchaeus*
Today salvation has come to this house.

Luke 19:9 ESV

*To some Pharisees*
I tell you, if these become silent, the stones will cry out!

Luke 19:40 NASB

*To the criminal on the cross*
Truly, I say to you, today you will be with me in paradise.

Luke 23:43 ESV

*To some Jews*
Destroy this temple, and in three days I will raise it up.

John 2:19 NKJV

*To the woman at the well*
I AM the Messiah!

John 4:26 NLT

*To a royal official*
Go; your son will live.

John 4:50 ESV

*To Jewish leaders*

For the Father loves the Son, and shows Him all things that He Himself is doing; and the Father will show Him greater works than these, so that you will marvel.

John 5:20 NASB

*To crowds in Capernaum who had been looking for Jesus*

Don't work for the food that perishes but for the food that lasts for eternal life, which the Son of Man will give you.

John 6:27 CSB

*To the crowds at Capernaum*

For the bread of God is the one who comes down from heaven and gives life to the world.

JOHN 6:33 CSB

*To the people in the temple courts*
I am going away, and you will seek me, and you will die in your sin. Where I am going, you cannot come.

John 8:21 ESV

*To believing Jews*
If you abide in My word, you are My disciples indeed. And you shall know the truth, and the truth shall make you free.

John 8:31–32 NKJV

*To believing Jews*
Therefore if the Son makes you free, you shall be free indeed.

John 8:36 NKJV

*To a man Jesus had healed from blindness*
You have seen him; in fact, he is the one speaking with you.

John 9:37 CSB

*To Mary and Martha*
This illness does not lead to death. It is for the glory of God, so that the Son of God may be glorified through it.

John 11:4 ESV

*To Mary and Martha*
Your brother will rise again.

John 11:23 ESV

*To a crowd of Greeks*

The light will be with you for a little longer, so walk while you have the light. Then the darkness will not catch you. If you walk in the darkness, you will not know where you are going. Believe in the light while you still have it so that you will become children of light.

John 12:35–36 NCV

*To Saul at his conversion*

Get up and go into Damascus, and there you will be told everything that you have been assigned to do.

Acts 22:10 CSB

*To Saul*
Go, for I will send you far away to the Gentiles.

Acts 22:21 ESV

*To Paul*
Be of good cheer, Paul; for as you have testified for Me in Jerusalem, so you must also bear witness at Rome.

Acts 23:11 NKJV

*To Paul*
My grace is sufficient for you, for My strength is made perfect in weakness.

2 Corinthians 12:9 NKJV

*To the church at Smyrna*
Do not fear what you are about to suffer. Behold, the devil is about to throw some of you into prison, that you may be tested, and for ten days you will have tribulation. Be faithful unto death, and I will give you the crown of life.

Revelation 2:10 ESV

*To the church at Thyatira*
Now I say to the rest of you in Thyatira, to you who do not hold to her teaching and have not learned Satan's so-called deep secrets, "I will not impose any other burden on you, except to hold on to what you have until I come."

Revelation 2:24–25 NIV

*To the church at Sardis*
Remember, then, what you received and heard.
Keep it, and repent. If you will not wake up, I will
come like a thief, and you will not know at what
hour I will come against you.

Revelation 3:3 ESV

*To the church at Sardis*
Yet you have still a few names in Sardis, people
who have not soiled their garments, and they will
walk with me in white, for they are worthy.

Revelation 3:4 ESV

*To the church at Philadelphia*
I know your works. Behold, I have set before you an open door, which no one is able to shut. I know that you have but little power, and yet you have kept my word and have not denied my name. Behold, I will make those of the synagogue of Satan who say that they are Jews and are not, but lie—behold, I will make them come and bow down before your feet, and they will learn that I have loved you.

Revelation 3:8–9 ESV

*To the church at Philadelphia*
Because you have kept my word about patient endurance, I will keep you from the hour of trial that is coming on the whole world, to try those who dwell on the earth.

Revelation 3:10 ESV

*To the church at Philadelphia*

I am coming soon.

**REVELATION 3:11** NIV

# ABOUT THE BIBLE TRANSLATIONS

G rateful thanks and acknowledgment are given to the following copyright holders for the Bible translations used in the compiling of this book:

Scripture quotations marked CSB have been taken from the Christian Standard Bible®, Copyright © 2017 by Holman Bible Publishers. Used by permission. Christian Standard Bible® and CSB® are federally registered trademarks of Holman Bible Publishers, all rights reserved.

Scripture quotations marked ESV are from the ESV® Bible (The Holy Bible, English Standard Version®), copyright © 2001 by Crossway Bibles, a publishing ministry of Good News Publishers. Used by permission. All rights reserved.

# Help us get the word out!

Our Daily Bread Publishing exists to feed the soul with the Word of God.

## If you appreciated this book, please let others know.

- Pick up another copy to give as a gift.
- Share a link to the book or mention it on social media.
- Write a review on your blog, on a bookseller's website, or at our own site (odb.org/store).
- Recommend this book for your church, book club, or small group.

## Connect with us:

📘 @ourdailybread

📷 @ourdailybread

🐦 @ourdailybread

Our Daily Bread Publishing
PO Box 3566
Grand Rapids, Michigan 49501 USA

✉ books@odb.org